BRITISH ARMY COLLAR BADGES
1881 TO THE PRESENT
An illustrated reference guide
for collectors

BRITISH ARMY COLLAR BADGES

1881 TO THE PRESENT

An illustrated reference guide
for collectors

Colin Churchill and
Ray Westlake

ARMS AND ARMOUR PRESS
LONDON NEW YORK SYDNEY

First published in Great Britain
in 1986 by Arms and Armour Press Limited,
2–6 Hampstead High Street, London NW3 1QQ.
Distributed in the USA by Sterling Publishing Co. Inc.,
2 Park Avenue, New York, N.Y. 10016.
Distributed in Australia by
Capricorn Link (Australia) Pty. Ltd., P.O. Box 665,
Lane Cove, New South Wales 2066, Australia.

ISBN 0-85368-895-8

Designed and edited by David Gibbons;
typeset by Typesetters (Birmingham) Limited;
printed and bound in Great Britain.

CONTENTS

INTRODUCTION

The collecting of military badges has for many years been a favourite pastime of both young and old alike. Initially it was the cap badge that was most popular among collectors, who would usually give little or no attention to other regimental badges. However, as time went on, hitherto neglected items such as buttons, shoulder titles and collar badges, became widely collected, and now form important parts of general or specialist collections.

As interest in the hobby grew, the need for reference books on the subject naturally arose. Cap and other head-dress insignia have already been covered, as have buttons, shoulder titles and the arm badges that denote the trade or proficiency of a soldier. Until now, however, the collar badge has never been dealt with; except for a few magazine articles, it has remained totally ignored in print.

Metal badges worn on the collar were introduced for infantry regiments in 1874, and at first were used only by privates and non commissioned officers. The requirement for some method of identification on uniform had arisen in 1871, when identifiable regimental buttons were replaced by a general service pattern bearing the Royal Arms. In 1874 a number of regiments were already in possession of approved badges, and these were authorized for use on the collar in a General Order issued on 30 June. Those units that had no badge were directed to adopt an Imperial Crown device.

Metal collar badges were to be fixed midway between the top and bottom of the collar, and with the centre of the badge 2 inches from the opening. When animals or birds are represented, they normally face inwards towards the opening of the collar; in the case of bugles, these are worn with the mouthpiece of the instrument also at the collar opening.

At this time no collar badges were authorized for the 60th Foot, Rifle Brigade, cavalry regiments, Royal Artillery (except for NCOs), Royal Engineers or the Army Service Corps. The three regiments of Foot Guards wore embroidered collar badges. After

1881, an opportunity for officers to wear collar badges arose when in that year their badges of rank, hitherto worn on the collar, were moved to the shoulder cords. The cavalry were also to adopt collar badges, and by the turn of the century almost all the British Army were wearing collar insignia on one form of dress or another. In this illustrated guide to collar badge collecting we have attempted to show at least one item each for the majority of the regular regiments of cavalry and infantry of the British Army since 1881. Also included are sections for the Arms and Services, the Yeomanry and other auxiliary forces, together with items worn by schools and training organizations and formations that existed only in time of war. All the items shown are made of metal and are representative of basic collar badge patterns. No attempt has been made either to illustrate the numerous variations that exist for the majority of badges, or to record the several metals in which most items have been manufactured.

In captioning the badges, we have started with the title of the unit; this is followed by a date, if relevant; the type of crown, if any; and the metal of the item illustrated. The system of dating a badge by the type of crown that it bears is widely used among collectors. The Queen Victoria Crown (Q.V.C.) was followed after her death by the King's Crown (K.C.) and then in 1952 by the Queen Elizabeth pattern (Q.E.C.). For the purpose of this book, crown changes have not been considered in the dating of badges. All the badges are reproduced at life size.

It is hoped that this book will provide the more recent collector, or those just branching out into collar badges, with a good idea as to what can be acquired. Tracking these down should provide a number of years of pleasure. Good hunting!

PRICE GUIDE

In pricing the items illustrated, we can only state what we as collectors have personally paid or would be willing to pay. While many of the collar badges illustrated are quite common and relatively inexpensive, others are more difficult to obtain; a few are quite scarce and even rare. This is, of course, reflected in the price. When a collar badge is also used as a cap badge, then the price as a cap badge is usually the one that is asked. This is reflected in the price guide. The figures quoted are for similar badges to those illustrated, in the same metals and for examples in near mint condition. Worn or damaged specimens would be of less value.

1.	£2	31.	£5	61.	£5
2.	£3	32.	£4	62.	£4
3.	£3	33.	£6	63.	£5
4.	£2	34.	£5	64.	£3
5.	£5	35.	£8	65.	£4
6.	£5	36.	£4	66.	£10
7.	£2	37.	£7.50	67.	£4
8.	£7.50	38.	£4	68.	£4
9.	£1.50	39.	£6	69.	£3
10.	£5	40.	£8	70.	£4
11.	£4	41.	£5	71.	£8
12.	£4	42.	£6	72.	£4
13.	£5	43.	£6	73.	£6
14.	£3	44.	£8	74.	£6
15.	£3	45.	£10	75.	£5
16.	£7.50	46.	£10	76.	£6
17.	£6	47.	£3	77.	£5
18.	£2	48.	£5	78.	£5
19.	£4	49.	£4	79.	£2.50
20.	£5	50.	£5	80.	£4
21.	£4	51.	£6	81.	£3
22.	£5	52.	£0.50	82.	£5
23.	£8	53.	£4	83.	£3.50
24.	£2	54.	£0.50	84.	£5
25.	£7	55.	£5	85.	£3
26.	£7.50	56.	£4	86.	£5
27.	£5	57.	£3	87.	£6
28.	£5	58.	£3	88.	£2.50
29.	£3.50	59.	£3	89.	£5
30.	£8	60.	£4	90.	£2.50

91. £8	149. £3	207. £3
92. £5	150. £3	208. £5
93. £3	151. £3	209. £2
94. £5	152. £3	210. £3
95. £5	153. £2	211. £5
96. £2	154. £7	212. £5
97. £4	155. £4	213. £2
98. £7	156. £6	214. £4
99. £2	157. £2	215. £1.50
100. £3	158. £4	216. £3
101. £6	159. £6	217. £2
102. £6	160. £6	218. £2
103. £4	161. £2.50	219. £3
104. £12	162. £2	220. £4
105. £3	163. £2	221. £4.50
106. £4	164. £3.50	222. £2.50
107. £6	165. £4	223. £3
108. £2.50	166. £2	224. £1.50
109. £6	167. £3	225. £2
110. £5	168. £2	226. £2
111. £4	169. £6	227. £2
112. £8	170. £3	228. £4
113. £5	171. £2	229. £3
114. £10	172. £6	230. £6
115. £8	173. £4	231. £5
116. £6	174. £3	232. £2
117. £3	175. £4	233. £3
118. £15	176. £3	234. £0.50
119. £5	177. £5	235. £5
120. £5	178. £1.50	236. £2
121. £5	179. £3	237. £3
122. £3	180. £3	238. £1.50
123. £5	181. £2	239. £3
124. £5	182. £4	240. £5
125. £5	183. £3	241. £5
126. £5	184. £2	242. £5
127. £0.50	185. £3	243. £3
128. £0.50	186. £3	244. £2
129. £0.50	187. £2	245. £4
130. £2	188. £4	246. £6
131. £4	189. £0.50	247. £5
132. £3	190. £5	248. £5
133. £2.50	191. £2.50	249. £3
134. £2	192. £1.50	250. £1.50
135. £2	193. £2	251. £2
136. £3	194. £3	252. £3.50
137. £5	195. £2	253. £2.50
138. £3	196. £5	254. £2
139. £2	197. £3.50	255. £4
140. £2.50	198. £7	256. £0.50
141. £3	199. £5	257. £3
142. £3	200. £3	258. £4
143. £5	201. £1.50	259. £7
144. £3	202. £4	260. £5
145. £2	203. £5	261. £1.50
146. £8	204. £3	262. £2.50
147. £8	205. £4	263. £2.50
148. £3	206. £2	264. £3

265. £2	319. £5	373. £2
266. £3	320. £5	374. £4
267. £3	321. £15	375. £2.50
268. £10	322. £3.50	376. £2.50
269. £2	323. £3	377. £4
270. £5	324. £3	378. £4
271. £2	325. £4	379. £3
272. £5	326. £3	380. £4
273. £6	327. £3	381. £2.50
274. £4	328. £2	382. £2.50
275. £3	329. £12	383. £5
276. £7.50	330. £2.50	384. £3
277. £2.50	331. £2.50	385. £3
278. £3	332. £3.50	386. £3
279. £2.50	333. £3.50	387. £2.50
280. £2.50	334. £3	388. £1.50
281. £2.50	335. £3	389. £0.25
282. £2.50	336. £3	390. £2
283. £2.50	337. £4	391. £2
284. £2.50	338. £5	392. £8
285. £2.50	339. £5	393. £4
286. £2.50	340. £15	394. £5
287. £0.50	341. £6	395. £3
288. £4	342. £10	396. £4
289. £3	343. £5	397. £5
290. £0.50	344. £6	398. £5
291. £3	345. £4.50	399. £3
292. £0.50	346. £6	400. £2
293. £0.50	347. £6	401. £5
294. £0.50	348. £5	402. £5
295. £0.50	349. £1	403. £10
296. £0.50	350. £5	404. £6
297. £0.50	351. £2	405. £4
298. £2.50	352. £5	406. £5
299. £0.50	353. £3	407. £5
300. £2.50	354. £5	408. £4
301. £1	355. £3	409. £2
302. £7	356. £4	410. £3
303. £3	357. £3	411. £4
304. £6	358. £5	412. £4
305. £6	359. £10	413. £3.50
306. £2	360. £12	414. £3
307. £5	361. £2.50	415. £7
308. £0.50	362. £6	416. £4
309. £5	363. £3.50	417. £7
310. £0.50	364. £4	418. £10
311. £3	365. £5	419. £5
312. £2	366. £3	420. £3
313. £7	367. £4	421. £3
314. £3	368. £4	422. £10
315. £4	369. £2.50	423. £2
316. £3	370. £1.50	424. £2
317. £2.50	371. £2.50	425. £2
318. £3	372. £4	426. £2

BRITISH ARMY COLLAR BADGES
1881 TO THE PRESENT

1. 1st King's Dragoon Guards: Worn prior to 1915 and from 1938. Gilding metal.
2. 1st King's Dragoon Guards: 1915–38. K.C. Bi metal.
3. The Queen's Bays (2nd Dragoon Guards): K.C. Gilding metal. Also worn by 1st The Queen's Dragoon Guards.
4. 3rd Dragoon Guards (Prince of Wales's): Bi metal.
5. 3rd Dragoon Guards (Prince of Wales's): Officers' service dress. Bronze.
6. 3rd Carabiniers (Prince of Wales's Dragoon Guards): Silver and gilt.
7. 4th Royal Irish Dragoon Guards: White metal.
8. 5th Dragoon Guards (Princess Charlotte of Wales's): Q.V.C. Bi metal.
9. 5th Royal Inniskilling Dragoon Guards: Bi metal.
10. The Carabiniers (6th Dragoon Guards): K.C. Silver and gilt.
11. 7th Dragoon Guards (Princess Royal's): Gilding metal.
12. The Royal Dragoons (1st Dragoons): Silver and gilt.
13. The Royal Scots Greys (2nd Dragoons): Officers' service dress. Bronze.
14. The Royal Scots Greys (2nd Dragoons): White metal.
15. 3rd The King's Own Hussars: White metal.
16. 4th Queen's Own Hussars: Pre 1906. Q.V.C. Bi metal.
17. 4th Queen's Own Hussars: Post 1906. K.C. Silver and gilt.
18. 5th Royal Irish Lancers: K.C. Gilding metal.

31

32

33

34

35

36

19. The Inniskillings (6th Dragoons): White metal. **20.** 7th Queen's Own Hussars: Q.E.C. Silver and gilt. **21.** 8th King's Royal Irish Hussars: K.C. Bi metal. **22.** 9th Queen's Royal Lancers: K.C. Bronze. **23.** 10th Royal Hussars (Prince of Wales's Own): Silver and gilt. Also worn by The Royal Hussars. **24.** 11th Hussars (Prince Albert's Own): Gilding metal. **25.** 12th Royal Lancers (Prince of Wales's): Post 1903. K.C. Bi metal. **26.** 13th Hussars: Q.V.C. Bi metal. **27.** 14th King's Hussars: Pre 1915. White metal. **28.** 14th King's Hussars: Post 1915. K.C. Gilding metal. **29.** 15th The King's Hussars: K.C. Bi metal. Also worn by 15th/19th Hussars. **30.** 16th The Queen's Lancers: Pre 1905. Q.V.C. Bi metal. **31.** 16th The Queen's Lancers: Post 1905. K.C. Bronze. Also worn by 16th/5th Lancers until 1954. **32.** 17th Lancers (Duke of Cambridge's Own): White metal. Also worn by 17th/21st Lancers. **33.** 18th Royal Hussars (Queen Mary's Own): Pre 1911. K.C. Gilding metal. **34.** 18th Royal Hussars (Queen Mary's Own): Post 1911. K.C. White metal. **35.** 19th Royal Hussars (Queen Alexandra's Own): White metal. **36.** 20th Hussars: K.C. Gilding metal.

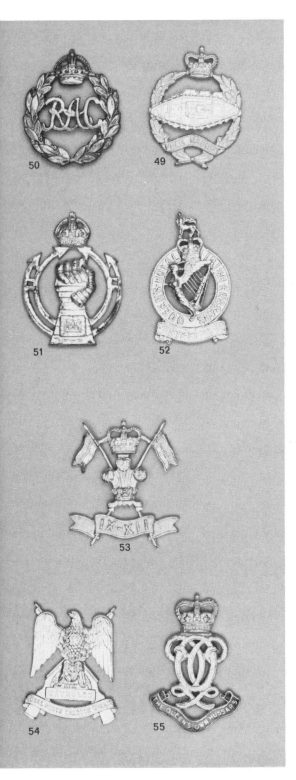

37. 21st Lancers (Empress of India's): Q.V.C. Bi metal.
38. 13th/18th Royal Hussars (Queen Mary's Own): Post 1938. Q.E.C. Gilding metal.
39. 14th/20th King's Hussars: K.C. Gilt.
40. 4th/7th Royal Dragoon Guards: Silver and gilt with red, white and blue enamel.
41. 22nd Dragoons: White metal.
42. 23rd Hussars: K.C. White metal.
43. 24th Lancers: K.C. Bronze.
44. 25th Dragoons: K.C. Bi metal.
45. 26th Hussars: Gilding metal.
46. 27th Lancers: K.C. Bi metal.
47. 16th/5th The Queen's Royal Lancers: Post 1954. Q.E.C. White metal.
48. Tank Corps: K.C. Gilding metal.
49. Royal Tank Corps, from 1939 – Royal Tank Regiment: Q.E.C. Silver and gilt.
50. Royal Armoured Corps: Pre 1941. K.C. Gilding metal.
51. Royal Armoured Corps: Post 1941. K.C. Silver plate.
52. The Queen's Royal Irish Hussars: Q.E.C. Gold and silver anodised aluminium.
53. 9th/12th Royal Lancers (Prince of Wales's): Q.E.C. Silver and gilt.
54. The Royal Scots Dragoon Guards (Carabiniers and Greys): Silver and gold anodised aluminium.
55. The Queen's Own Hussars: Silver plate, gilt and blue enamel.

56

57

58

59

61

60

63

62

65

64

67

66

68

56. Royal Wiltshire Yeomanry (Prince of Wales's Own): Bronze.
57. Warwickshire Yeomanry: Gilding metal.
58. Yorkshire Hussars (Alexandra, Princess of Wales's Own): Bi metal.
59. Nottinghamshire (Sherwood Rangers) Yeomanry: Pre 1949. Gilding metal.
60. Nottinghamshire (Sherwood Rangers) Yeomanry: Post 1949. K.C. Gilding metal.
61. Staffordshire Yeomanry (Queen's Own Royal Regiment): Q.V.C. Officers' service dress pattern. Bronze.
62. Shropshire Yeomanry: Q.E.C. Gilding metal.
63. Ayrshire (Earl of Carrick's Own) Yeomanry: Silver and gilt.
64. Cheshire Yeomanry (Earl of Chester's): Bronze.
65. Queen's Own Yorkshire Dragoons: K.C. Gilding metal.
66. Leicestershire Yeomanry (Prince Albert's Own): Pre 1908. K.C. White metal.
67. North Somerset Yeomanry: K.C. George V Royal Cypher. White metal.
68. Duke of Lancaster's Own Yeomanry: Bronze.
69. Northumberland Hussars: K.C. White metal.
70. South Nottinghamshire Hussars: White metal.
71. Denbighshire Hussars: Bronze.
72. Westmorland and Cumberland Yeomanry: K.C. Gilding metal.
73. Pembroke Yeomanry: Silver and gilt.
74. Royal East Kent Yeomanry: K.C. Bronze.
75. Hampshire Carabiniers Yeomanry: K.C. Bi metal.
76. Royal Buckinghamshire Hussars: K.C. Gilding metal.

77. Derbyshire Yeomanry: K.C. Bronze.
78. Queen's Own Dorsetshire Yeomanry: K.C. George V. Bronze.
79. Royal Gloucestershire Hussars: Gilding metal.
80. Hertfordshire Yeomanry: Gilding metal.
81. Berkshire Yeomanry: Gilding metal.
82. Berkshire Yeomanry: Bronze.
83. Duke of York's Own Loyal Suffolk Hussars: White metal.
84. Royal First Devonshire Yeomanry: K.C. Bronze.
85. Middlesex Yeomanry: Post 1952. Q.E.C. Bi metal.
86. Royal North Devonshire Hussars: K.C. White metal.
87. Queen's Own Worcestershire Hussars: K.C. Silver and gilt.
88. West Kent Yeomanry (Queen's Own): White metal.
89. West Somerset Yeomanry: Bronze.
90. Queen's Own Oxfordshire Hussars: Queen Adelaide's Crown. White metal.
91. Montgomeryshire Yeomanry: Pre 1900. Bronze.
92. Lancashire Hussars: Bronze.
93. Lothians and Border Horse: Gilding metal.
94. Queen's Own Royal Glasgow Yeomanry: K.C. Gilding metal.
95. Surrey Yeomanry (Queen Mary's Regiment): Post 1910. K.C. White metal.
96. Fife and Forfar Yeomanry: White metal.

97

98

100

101

103

104

105

106

107

108

FORRARD

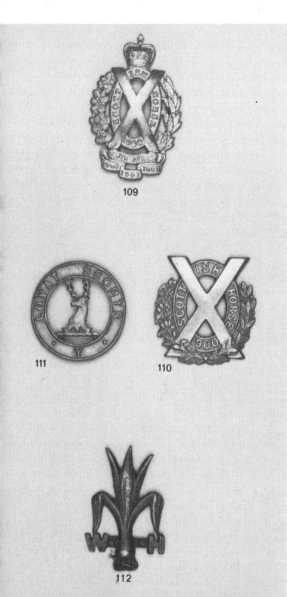

97. Sussex Yeomanry: K.C.
Gilding metal.
98. Norfolk Yeomanry, The
King's Own Royal Regiment:
K.C. Gilt.
99. Glamorgan Yeomanry:
White metal.
100. Lincolnshire Yeomanry:
White metal.
101. City of London Yeomanry
(Rough Riders): Silver gilt.
102. 2nd County of London
Yeomanry (Westminster
Dragoons): Gilt.
103. 3rd and 3/4th County of
London Yeomanry (Sharp-
shooters): 1939–61. K.C.
Gilding metal.
104. Bedfordshire Yeomanry:
Bronze.
105. Northamptonshire Yeomanry: White metal.
106. Essex Yeomanry: K.C.
Gilding metal.
107. East Riding of Yorkshire
Yeomanry: Pre 1912. Gilding
metal.
108. East Riding of Yorkshire
Yeomanry: Post 1912. Bi
metal.
109. Scottish Horse: Post 1903.
Gilt.
110. Scottish Horse: Pre 1903.
Gilding metal.
111. Lovat Scouts: Post 1908.
Gilding metal.
112. Welsh Horse: Bronze.
113. 4th County of London
Yeomanry (Sharpshooters):
1939–44. Bi metal.
114. 4th County of London
(King's Colonials) Imperial
Yeomanry: 1st Pattern.
Gilding metal.

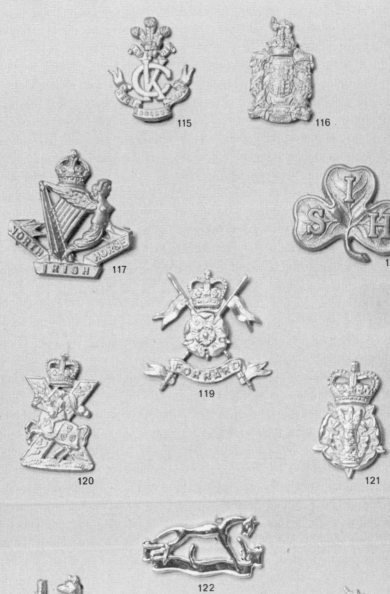

115

116

117

118

119

120

121

122

123

124

115. 4th County of London (King's Colonials) Imperial Yeomanry: 2nd pattern. Gilt.
116. King Edward's Horse (The King's Overseas Dominions Regiment): K.C. Yellow brass.
117. North Irish Horse: Post 1908. K.C. Gilding metal.
118. South Irish Horse: Post 1908. Gilt.
119. Queen's Own Yorkshire Yeomanry: Q.E.C. Silver plate.
120. Fife and Forfar Yeomanry/Scottish Horse: Q.E.C. Silver plate.
121. Leicestershire and Derbyshire (Prince Albert's Own) Yeomanry: Q.E.C. Silver and gilt.
122. Berkshire and Westminster Dragoons: Gold anodised aluminium.
123. Queen's Own Warwickshire and Worcestershire Yeomanry: Silver plate.
124. Queen's Own Lowland Yeomanry: Silver and gilt.
125. Inns of Court and City Yeomanry: Silver and gilt.
126. Suffolk and Norfolk Yeomanry: Q.E.C. Silver and gilt.
127. Flintshire and Denbighshire Yeomanry: Gold and silver anodised aluminium.
128. Queen's Own Dorset and West Somerset Yeomanry: Q.E.C. Gold and silver anodised aluminium.
129. Kent and County of London Yeomanry: Q.E.C. Gold and silver anodised aluminium.

130

131

132

133

134

135

136

137

138

139

140

130. The Royal Scots (The Royal Regiment): Gilding metal.
131. The Royal Scots (The Royal Regiment): Officers service dress pattern. Bronze.
132. The Queen's Royal Regiment (West Surrey): Early pattern. Gilding metal.
133. The Queen's Royal Regiment (West Surrey): Pre 1920. Bi metal.
134. The Queen's Royal Regiment (West Surrey): Post 1920. Gilding metal.
135. The Buffs (Royal East Kent Regiment): Gilding metal.
136. The Buffs (Royal East Kent Regiment): Officers' service dress pattern. Bronze.
137. The King's Own Royal Regiment (Lancaster): 1881–4. Gilt.
138. The King's Own Royal Regiment (Lancaster): Officers' service dress. Bronze.
139. The King's Own Royal Regiment (Lancaster): Post 1884. Gilding metal.
140. The Royal Northumberland Fusiliers: Pre 1949. Gilding metal.
141. The Royal Northumberland Fusiliers: Officers' pattern. Bronze.
142. The Royal Warwickshire Regiment: Early pattern. Gilding metal.
143. The Royal Warwickshire Regiment: Silver and gilt.
144. The Royal Warwickshire Regiment: Officers' service dress pattern. Bronze.
145. The Royal Fusiliers (City of London Regiment): Q.V.C. Gilding metal.
146. The Royal Fusiliers (City of London Regiment): Officers' pattern. Silver and gilt.

29

147

148

149

150

151

152

153

154

155

156

157

158

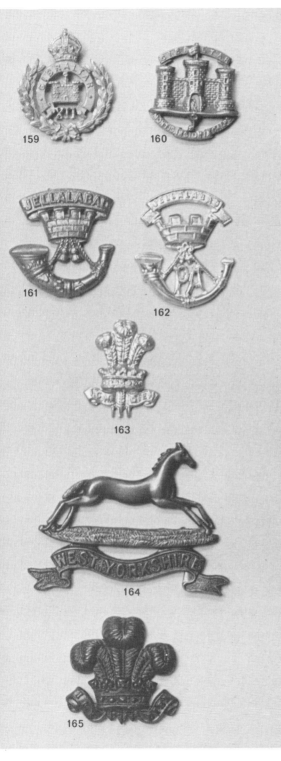

147. The King's Regiment (Liverpool): 1882–95. Gilt and enamel.
148. The King's Regiment (Liverpool): 1895–1926. Bi metal.
149. The King's Regiment (Liverpool): Post 1926. Officers' service dress. Bronze.
150. The Royal Norfolk Regiment: Officers' service dress. Bronze.
151. The Norfolk Regiment: Pre 1935. Officers' service dress. Bronze.
152. The Lincolnshire Regiment: Pre 1946. Officers' service dress. Bronze.
153. The Royal Lincolnshire Regiment: White metal.
154. The Royal Lincolnshire Regiment: Post 1946. Officers' pattern. Silver, gilt and blue enamel.
155. The Devonshire Regiment: Early pattern. Gilding metal.
156. The Devonshire Regiment: K.C. Silver, gilt and blue enamel.
157. The Suffolk Regiment: Pre 1902. Gilding metal.
158. The Suffolk Regiment: Gilt.
159. The Suffolk Regiment: K.C. Gilt. Worn on No. 3 dress and tropical mess dress.
160. The Suffolk Regiment: Silver and gilt.
161. The Somerset Light Infantry (Prince Albert's): Early type. Gilding metal.
162. The Somerset Light Infantry (Prince Albert's): Post 1948. White metal.
163. The West Yorkshire Regiment (The Prince of Wales's Own): Bi metal.
164. The West Yorkshire Regiment (The Prince of Wales's Own): Pre 1925. Officers' service dress. Bronze.
165. The West Yorkshire Regiment (The Prince of Wales's Own): Post 1925. Officers' service dress. Bronze.

166

167

168

169

170

171

172

173

174

175

176

177

166. The East Yorkshire Regiment (The Duke of York's Own): Bi metal.
167. The East Yorkshire Regiment (The Duke of York's Own): Officers' service dress. Bronze.
168. The Bedfordshire Regiment: Bi metal.
169. The Bedfordshire Regiment: Pre 1919. Officers' type. Silver and gilt.
170. The Bedfordshire Regiment: Pre 1919. Officers' service dress. Bronze.
171. The Bedfordshire and Hertfordshire Regiment: Post 1919. Bi metal.
172. The Bedfordshire and Hertfordshire Regiment: Post 1919. Silver and gilt and blue enamel.
173. The Royal Leicestershire Regiment: Pre 1951. Silver and gilt.
174. The Leicestershire Regiment: Pre 1946. Officers' service dress. Bronze.
175. The Royal Leicestershire Regiment: Post 1951. Silver and gilt.
176. The Royal Irish Regiment: Gilding metal.
177. The Royal Irish Regiment: Silver.
178. The Green Howards (Alexandra Princess of Wales's Own Yorkshire Regiment): Gilding metal.
179. The Green Howards (Alexandra Princess of Wales's Own Yorkshire Regiment): Officers' service dress. Bronze.
180. The Lancashire Fusiliers: Officers' service dress. Bronze.
181. The Lancashire Fusiliers: Gilding metal. Also worn by Royal Welch Fusiliers and Royal Munster Fusiliers.
182. The Lancashire Fusiliers: Silver and gilt.
183. The Lancashire Fusiliers: Officers' service dress. Bronze.

33

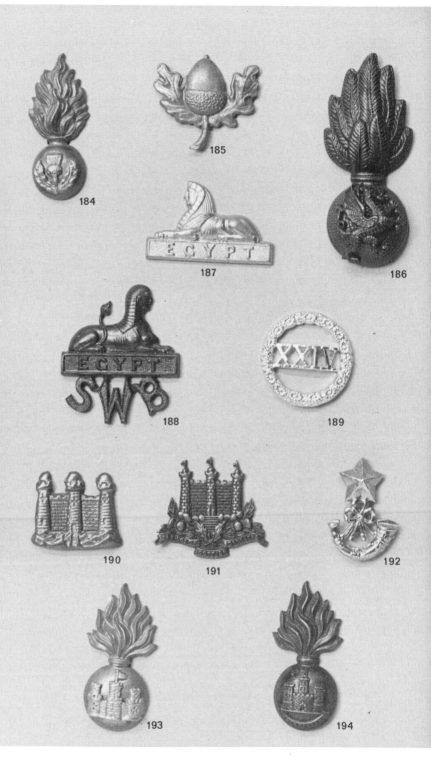

184. The Royal Scots Fusiliers.
Bi metal.
185. The Cheshire Regiment:
Gilding metal.
186. The Royal Welsh
Fusiliers: Officers' service
dress. Bronze.
187. The South Wales
Borderers: Pre 1957. White
metal.
188. The South Wales
Borderers: Officers' service
dress. Bronze.
189. The South Wales
Borderers: Post 1957. Silver
anodised aluminium.
190. The King's Own Scottish
Borderers: Pre 1887. Gilding
metal.
191. The King's Own Scottish
Borderers: Post 1887. Bronze.
192. The Cameronians
(Scottish Rifles): White metal.
193. The Royal Inniskilling
Fusiliers: Bi metal.
194. The Royal Inniskilling
Fusiliers: Bronze.
195. The Gloucestershire Regiment: Pre 1957. White metal.
196. The Gloucestershire Regiment: Post 1957. Gilt.
197. The Gloucestershire Regiment: Officers' service dress.
Bronze.
198. The Worcestershire Regiment: c.1890. Silver and gilt.
199. The Worcestershire Regiment: Pre 1925. Silver and gilt.
200. The Worcestershire Regiment: Pre 1925. Officers'
service dress. Bronze.

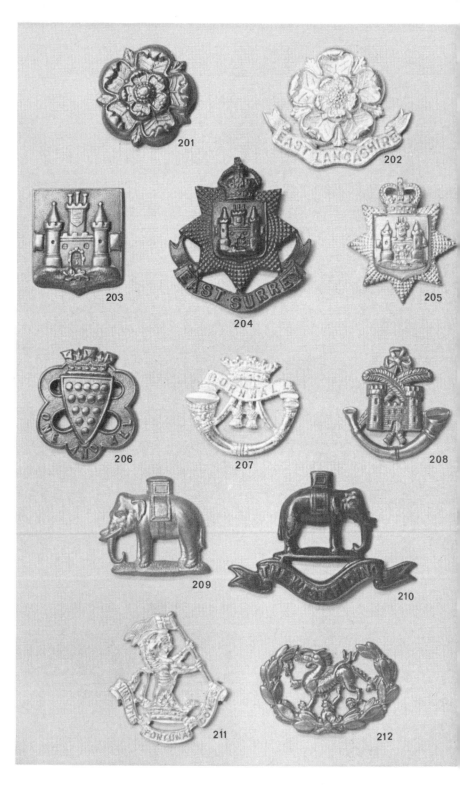

201. The East Lancashire
Regiment: Gilding metal.
202. The East Lancashire
Regiment: Officers' pattern.
Silver plate.
203. The East Surrey Regiment: Early pattern. Silver and
gilt.
204. The East Surrey Regiment: Officers' service dress.
K.C. Bronze.
205. The East Surrey Regiment: Q.E.C. Silver and gilt.
206. The Duke of Cornwall's
Light Infantry: Post 1884.
Gilding metal.
207. The Duke of Cornwall's
Light Infantry: Post 1932.
Silver plate.
208. The Duke of Cornwall's
Light Infantry: Pre 1884.
Gilding metal.
209. The Duke of Wellington's
Regiment (West Riding): Pre
1958. Reintroduced 1969.
Gilding metal.
210. The Duke of Wellington's
Regiment (West Riding):
Officers' service dress. Bronze.
211. The Duke of Wellington's
Regiment (West Riding):
1958–69. Silver plate.
212. The Border Regiment:
Pre 1884. Gilding metal.
213. The Border Regiment:
Post 1884. Gilding metal.
214. The Border Regiment:
Post 1895. Silver plate and
enamel.
215. The Royal Sussex Regiment: Gilding metal.
216. The Royal Sussex Regiment: Officers' service dress.
Bronze.
217. The Royal Hampshire
Regiment: Gilding metal.
218. The South Staffordshire
Regiment: Gilding metal.

219. Dorset Regiment: Officers' service dress. Bronze.
220. South Lancashire Regiment (The Prince of Wales's Volunteers): Pre 1956. Silver and gilt.
221. South Lancashire Regiment (The Prince of Wales's Volunteers): Post 1956. Silver and gilt.
222. Welch Regiment: Pre 1950. White metal.
223. Welch Regiment: Officers' service dress. Bronze. Worn by other ranks in white metal after 1951.
224. Black Watch (Royal Highlanders Regiment): White metal.
225. Oxfordshire and Buckinghamshire Light Infantry: Worn by service battalions 1914–18. Black metal.
226. Oxfordshire and Buckinghamshire Light Infantry: Regimental button worn by Officers on the collar.
227. The Essex Regiment. Bronze.
228. Essex Regiment: Post 1954. Gilding metal. Prior to this No. 227 without the scroll was worn.
229. Sherwood Foresters (Nottinghamshire and Derbyshire Regiment): Post 1902. K.C. Officers' service dress. Bronze.
230. Sherwood Foresters (Derbyshire Regiment): Pre 1902. Q.V.C. Silver and gilt with blue enamel.
231. Loyal Regiment (North Lancashire): Q.V.C. Gilding metal.
232. Loyal Regiment (North Lancashire): Pre 1957. Gilding metal.
233. Loyal Regiment (North Lancashire): Pre 1957. Officers' service dress. Bronze.
234. Loyal Regiment (North Lancashire): Post 1957. Q.E.C. Gold anodised aluminium.
235. Northamptonshire Regiment: Q.E.C. Silver gilt and enamel.
236. Royal Berkshire Regiment (Princess Charlotte of Wales's): Gilding metal.
237. Royal Berkshire Regiment (Princess Charlotte of Wales's): Officers' service dress. Bronze.

238

239

ROYAL KENT WEST

240

KING'S OWN

241

242

243

KSLI

244

245

MIDDLESEX REGT

246

247

248

249

MANCHESTER

250

251

252

253

238. The Queen's Own Royal West Kent Regiment: K.C. Gilding metal.
239. The Queen's Own Royal West Kent Regiment: Officers' service dress. K.C. Bronze.
240. The King's Own Yorkshire Light Infantry: Pre 1887. Gilding metal.
241. The King's Own Yorkshire Light Infantry: Post 1887. Silver and black.
242. The King's Shropshire Light Infantry: 1881–1882. Gilding metal.
243. The King's Shropshire Light Infantry: Officers' type. Bronze. Smaller version worn by other ranks in bi metal from 1952.
244. The Middlesex Regiment (Duke of Cambridge's Own): Bi metal.
245. The Middlesex Regiment (Duke of Cambridge's Own): Officers' service dress. Bronze.
246. The Middlesex Regiment (Duke of Cambridge's Own): Officers' type. Silver and gilt.
247. The Wiltshire Regiment (The Duke of Edinburgh's): Pre 1956. Silver and gilt.
248. The Wiltshire Regiment (The Duke of Edinburgh's): Post 1956. Silver and gilt.
249. The Manchester Regiment: Pre 1923. Officers' service dress. Bronze.
250. The Manchester Regiment: Pre 1923. White metal.
251. The Manchester Regiment: Post 1923. Gilding metal.
252. The North Staffordshire Regiment (The Prince of Wales's) 1895–c.1902: Bi metal.
253. The North Staffordshire Regiment (The Prince of Wales's): Post 1902. Bi metal.

254

255

256

257

258

259

260

261

262

263

264

265

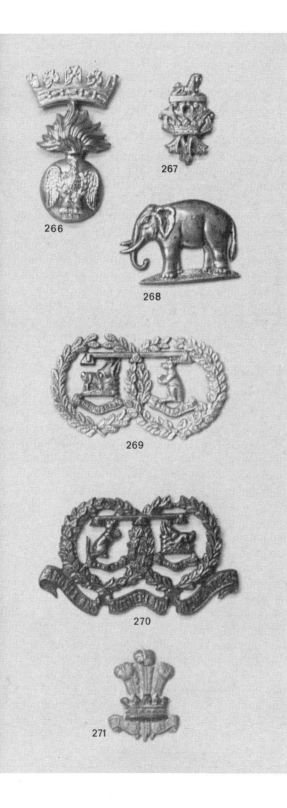

254. The York and Lancaster Regiment: Bi metal.
255. The York and Lancaster Regiment: Officers' service dress. Bronze.
256. The Durham Light Infantry: Q.E.C. Silver anodised aluminium.
257. The Highland Light Infantry (City of Glasgow Regiment): Q.V.C. White metal.
258. Seaforth Highlanders (Ross-shire Buffs, The Duke of Albany's): Officers' service dress. Bronze.
259. Seaforth Highlanders (Ross-shire Buffs, The Duke of Albany's): Gilt. This badge was worn with number 260 below, both being placed either side of the collar with number 260 nearest the opening.
260. Seaforth Highlanders (Ross-shire Buffs, The Duke of Albany's): Worn with number 259, see above. Gilt.
261. The Gordon Highlanders: White metal.
262. The Gordon Highlanders: Officers' pattern. Bronze.
263. The Queen's Own Cameron Highlanders: K.C. Bronze.
264. The Royal Ulster Rifles: Officers' service dress. K.C. Blackened brass.
265. The Royal Ulster Rifles: Q.E.C. Post 1957. Blackened metal.
266. The Royal Irish Fusiliers (Princess Victoria's): Bi metal.
267. The Royal Irish Fusiliers (Princess Victoria's): Early pattern. Gilding metal.
268. The Connaught Rangers: Silver.
269. The Argyll and Sutherland Highlanders (Princess Louise's): White metal.
270. The Argyll and Sutherland Highlanders (Princess Louise's): Officers' service dress. Bronze.
271. The Prince of Wales's Leinster Regiment (Royal Canadians): Bi metal.

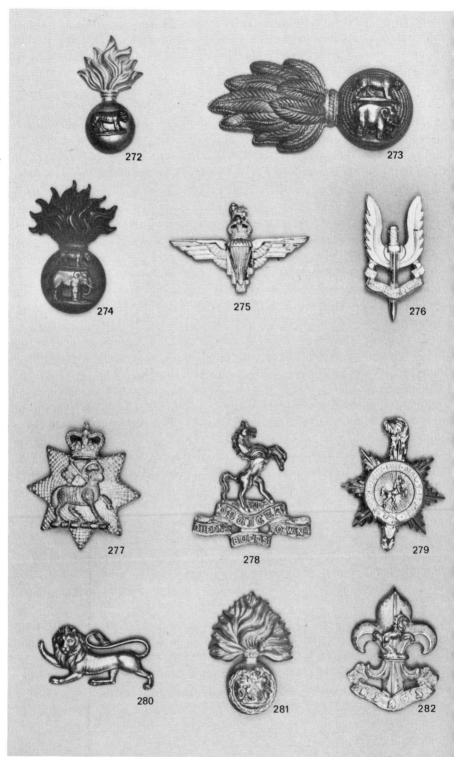

272

273

274

275

276

277

278

279

280

281

282

283

284

285

286

287

272. The Royal Munster Fusiliers: Silver and gilt.
273. The Royal Dublin Fusiliers: Officers' pattern. Silver and gilt.
274. The Royal Dublin Fusiliers: Officers' service dress. Bronze.
275. The Parachute Regiment: K.C. White metal.
276. The Special Air Service Regiment: Silver and gilt.
277. The Queen's Royal Surrey Regiment: Q.E.C. Silver and gilt.
278. The Queen's Own Buffs: Silver.
279. The Queen's Regiment: Silver and gilt.
280. The King's Own Royal Border Regiment: Silver.
281. The Royal Regiment of Fusiliers: Q.E.C. Silver and gilt.
282. The King's Regiment: Silver and gilt.
283. 1st Battalion, East, later Royal Anglian Regiment: Silver and gilt. 1959–64 and post c.1978.
284. 2nd Battalion, East, later Royal Anglian Regiment: Silver and gilt. 1960–64 and post c.1978.
285. 3rd Battalion, East, later Royal Anglian Regiment: Silver and gilt. 1958–64 and post c.1978.
286. 4th Battalion Royal Anglian Regiment: Silver and gilt.
287. The Royal Anglian Regiment: Gold and silver anodised aluminium. 1964–c.1978.

288

289

290

291

292

293

294

295

296

297

298

299

300

301

288. The Devon and Dorset Regiment: Silver and gilt.
289. The Somerset and Cornwall Light Infantry: Bronze.
290. The Light Infantry: Silver anodised aluminium.
291. The Prince of Wales's Own Regiment of Yorkshire: Silver, gilt and black enamel.
292. The Royal Highland Fusiliers: Gold and silver anodised aluminium.
293. The Royal Regiment of Wales: Silver anodised aluminium.
294. The Royal Irish Rangers: Silver anodised aluminium.
295. The Worcestershire and Sherwood Foresters Regiment: Gold and silver anodised aluminium.
296. The Lancashire Regiment (Prince of Wales's Volunteers): Gold and silver anodised aluminium.
297. The Queen's Lancashire Regiment: Gold anodised. Rose painted red.
298. The Staffordshire Regiment: Q.E.C. Silver and gilt.
299. The Duke of Edinburgh's Royal Regiment: Gold and silver anodised aluminium.
300. The Queen's Own Highlanders: Silver plate.
301. The Royal Green Jackets: Blackened metal.

302

303

304

305

306

307

308

309

310

311

312

302. Honourable Artillery Company: Bi metal.
303. Honourable Artillery Company: Officers' service dress. Bronze.
304. Northern Cyclist Battalion: K.C. Gilding metal.
305. 2nd Battalion, The Monmouthshire Regiment: Gilt.
306. The Cambridgeshire Regiment: White metal.
307. The Hertfordshire Regiment: Gilt.
308. The Bedfordshire and Hertfordshire Regiment (T.A.): Silver anodised aluminium.
309. The Herefordshire Regiment: 1915. Officers' service dress. Bronze.
310. The Herefordshire Light Infantry: Post 1964. Silver anodised aluminium.
311. The Herefordshire Regiment: 1908–64. White metal.
312. 1st to 4th Battalions, The London Regiment (Royal Fusiliers): K.C. Gilding metal.
313. 7th Battalion, The London Regiment: Gilding metal.
314. 8th Battalion, The London Regiment (Post Office Rifles): K.C. White metal.
315. 10th Battalion, The London Regiment (Hackney): K.C. Gilt.
316. 13th Battalion, The London Regiment (Kensington): White metal.
317. 13th Battalion, The London Regiment (Kensington): Post 1953. White metal.
318. 14th Battalion, The London Regiment (London Scottish): Officers' service dress. Bronze.
319. 15th Battalion, The London Regiment (Prince of Wales's Civil Service Rifles): White metal.
320. 16th Battalion, The London Regiment (Queen's Westminster Rifles): Q.V.C. Silver plated.

321

322

323

324

325

326

327

328

329

330

331

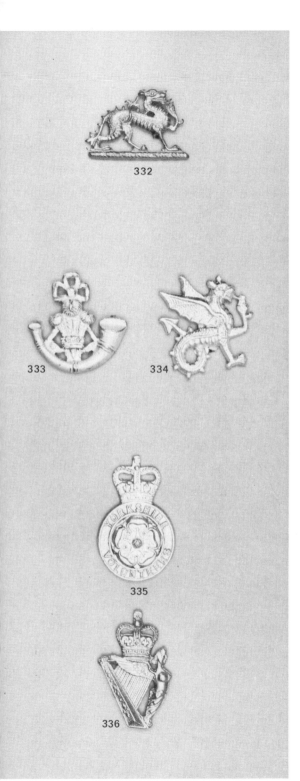

321. 16th Battalion, The London Regiment (Queen's Westminster and Civil Service Rifles): K.C. Gilt.
322. Tower Hamlets Rifle Volunteers: White metal.
323. 18th Battalion, The London Regiment (London Irish): Blackened brass.
324. 19th Battalion, The London Regiment (St. Pancras): Gilding metal.
325. 20th Battalion, The London Regiment (Blackheath and Woolwich): Officers' service dress. Bronze.
326. 22nd Battalion, The London Regiment(The Queen's): Pre 1908. White metal.
327. 23rd Battalion, The London Regiment: K.C. Bi metal.
328. 24th Battalion, The London Regiment (The Queen's): Gilding metal.
329. 25th Cyclist Battalion, The London Regiment: K.C. White metal.
330. 28th Battalion, The London Regiment (Artists Rifles): Gilding metal.
331. The Inns of Court Regiment: 1947–61. K.C. Gilding metal.
332. The Royal Berkshire Territorials: Gilt.
333. The Leeds Rifles: 1961–70. Silver and gilt.
334. The Wessex Regiment: Silver plate.
335. The Yorkshire Volunteers: Q.E.C. Silver anodised aluminium.
336. The Ulster Defence Regiment: Q.E.C. Gilt.

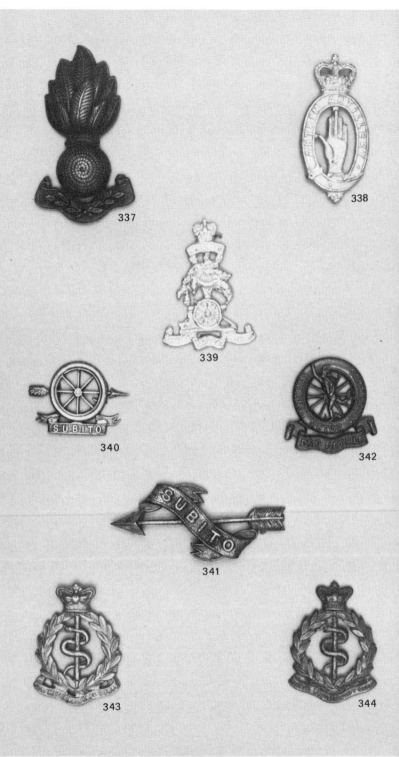

337

338

339

340

342

341

343

344

345

346

347

348

337. Royal Artillery, Territorials: Officers' service dress. Bronze.
338. Antrim Artillery: Q.E.C. Gilt.
339. 280th City of Glasgow Field Regiment, Royal Artillery: Q.E.C. Gilt.
340. Motor Volunteer Corps: Silver.
341. Army Motor Reserve: Bronze.
342. National Motor Volunteers: Bronze.
343. Volunteer Medical Staff Corps: Q.V.C. White metal.
344. Militia Medical Staff Corps: Q.V.C. Gilding metal.
345. Royal Army Medical Corps Volunteers: K.C. White metal.
346. 7th Battalion, Royal Hampshire Regiment: Gilding metal.
347. 6th (Fifeshire) Volunteer Battalion, The Black Watch: White metal.
348. 4th (Perthshire) Volunteer Battalion, The Black Watch: White metal.

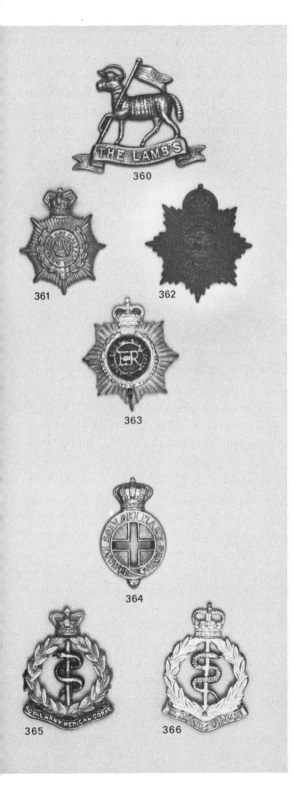

349. Royal Horse Artillery: Post 1970s. Q.E.C. Silver anodised.
350. Royal Artillery: Gilt.
351. Royal Engineers: Officers' service dress. Bronze.
352. Royal Corps of Signals: Pre 1946. K.C. Silver and gilt.
353. Royal Corps of Signals: Post 1946. Silver and gilt.
354. Army Air Corps: Pre 1950. Officers' service dress. Bronze.
355. Army Air Corps: Post 1961. Silver plate.
356. Glider Pilot Regiment: K.C. White metal.
357. Royal Army Chaplains' Department: (Christian). Pre 1940. K.C. Blackened metal.
358. Royal Army Chaplains' Department: (Christian). Post 1940. K.C. Silver, gilt and blue enamel.
359. Royal Army Chaplains' Department: (Jewish). Post 1940. K.C. Blackened metal.
360. Light Armoured Motor Batteries: 1916–19. Gilt.
361. Army Service Corps. Q.V.C. Gilding metal.
362. Royal Army Service Corps: K.C. Edward VIII cypher. Officers' service dress. Bronze.
363. Royal Corps of Transport: Q.E.C. Silver, gilt with red and blue enamel.
364. Medical Staff Corps: Q.V.C. Gilding metal.
365. Royal Army Medical Corps: Pre 1950. Q.V.C. Silver and gilt.
366. Royal Army Medical Corps: Post 1950. Q.E.C. Silver and gilt.

367

368

369

370

371

372

373

374

375

376

377

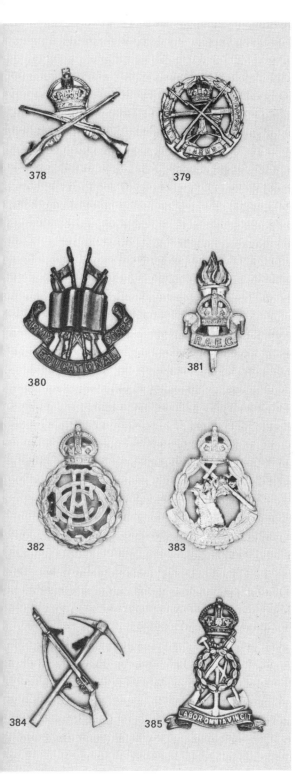

367. Army Ordnance Corps: Pre 1919. Bronze.
368. Royal Army Ordnance Corps: 1919–47. K.C. Silver, gilt and enamel.
369. Royal Army Ordnance Corps: Post 1949. K.C. Silver and gilt.
370. Royal Electrical and Mechanical Engineers: Pre 1947. K.C. Gilding metal.
371. Royal Electrical and Mechanical Engineers: Post 1947. K.C. Silver and gilt.
372. Royal Military Police: K.C. George VI cypher. Silver plate.
373. Army Pay Corps: 1902–20. Gilding metal.
374. Royal Army Pay Corps: 1920–29. K.C. Bronze.
375. Royal Army Pay Corps: Post 1929. K.C. Silver and gilt.
376. Army Veterinary Corps: Pre 1918. K.C. Gilding metal.
377. Royal Army Veterinary Corps: Post 1918. K.C. Bronze.
378. School of Musketry: K.C. Gilding metal.
379. Small Arms School Corps: K.C. Gilding metal.
380. Army Educational Corps: Pre 1948. Officers' service dress. Bronze.
381. Royal Army Educational Corps: Post 1948. K.C. Silver and gilt.
382. Army Dental Corps: Pre 1948. K.C. Gilding metal.
383. Royal Army Dental Corps: Post 1948. K.C. Silver and gilt.
384. Pioneer Units: Great War. Gilding metal.
385. Royal Pioneer Corps: K.C. Silver plate.

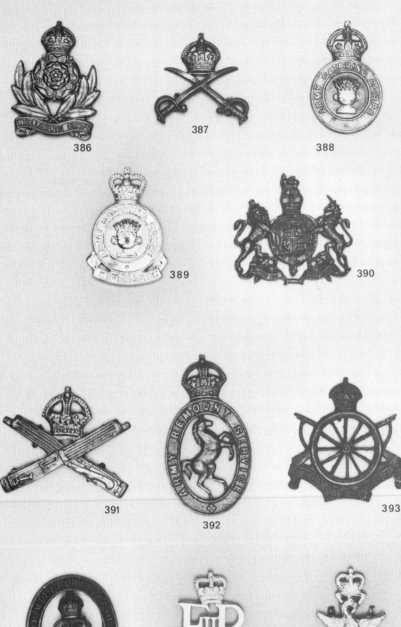

386

387

388

389

390

391

392

393

394

395

396

386. Intelligence Corps: K.C. Gilding metal.
387. Army Physical Training Corps: K.C. Gilding metal.
388. Army Catering Corps: Pre 1972. K.C. Bi metal.
389. Army Catering Corps: Post 1972. Q.E.C. Gold and silver anodised aluminium.
390. General Service Corps: Q.E.C. Bronze.
391. Machine Gun Corps: K.C. Gilding metal.
392. Army Remount Service: K.C. Officers' service dress. Bronze.
393. Army Cyclist Corps: K.C. Officers' service dress. Bronze.
394. Corps of Military Accountants: K.C. George V cypher. Bronze.
395. Military Provost Staff Corps: Q.E.C. Gilt.
396. Mobile Defence Corps: Q.E.C. Silver and gilt.
397. Reconnaissance Corps: Silver plate.
398. Royal Military Academy Sandhurst: K.C. George VI cypher. Silver plate.
399. Army Apprentices School: K.C. Gilding metal.
400. Welbeck College: Bi metal.
401. Royal Military College: K.C. George V cypher. Bronze.
402. Army Legal Services: Q.E.C. Silver plate with red and black enamels.
403. Army Scripture Readers: Bi metal.

 404

 405

 406

 407

 408

 409

 410

411

412

413

414

404. First Aid Nursing Yeomanry: Pre 1933. Bronze.
405. Women's Transport Service (F.A.N.Y.): Post 1933. Bronze.
406. Mechanized Transport Corps: Bronze.
407. Women's Army Auxiliary Corps: Bronze.
408. Queen Mary's Army Auxiliary Corps: K.C. Bronze.
409. Auxiliary Territorial Service: K.C. Bronze.
410. Women's Royal Army Corps: K.C. Gilt.
411. Queen Alexandra's Imperial Military Nursing Service: K.C. Silver and gilt.
412. Queen Alexandra's Imperial Military Nursing Service Reserve: K.C. Silver plate.
413. Queen Alexandra's Royal Army Nursing Corps: Q.E.C. Silver and gilt.
414. Territorial Army Nursing Service: K.C. Silver and gilt.

415

416

417

418

419

420

421

422

423

424

425

426

415. Royal Marine Artillery: Gilt.
416. Royal Marines: Silver and gilt.
417. Royal Naval Air Service, Armoured Car Section: K.C. Bronze.
418. Anson Battalion, Royal Naval Division: Gilding metal.
419. Royal Flying Corps: K.C. Bronze.
420. National Defence Companies: K.C. GVI cypher. Bronze.
421. Navy, Army and Air Force Institutes (NAAFI): K.C. Black metal.
422. Entertainments National Service Association (ENSA). Bronze.
423. Queen's University, Belfast Officers Training Corps: K.C. Bronze.
424. Edinburgh University Officers Training Corps: K.C. White metal.
425. University of London Officers Training Corps: K.C. Gilding metal.
426. Reading University College Officers Training Corps: Bronze.

INDEX